CONTENTS

PHOTO CREDITS
COVER PHOTOS BY GLEN S. AXELROD
Glen S. Axelrod: p. 14, 18, 26, 48, 60, 61, 70, 71, 74, 78, 79, 82, 83; B. Seed: p. 9, 33, 34, 37(4), 30, 31, 45, 49, 67, 76, 90(1), 91; Louise van der Meid: p. 8(2 & 3), 32, 33, 41-43, 46(1 & 2), 62, 72, 73; M.F. Roberts: p. 8(1), 16, 51, 69; Mrs. I. Routledge: p. 15, 27(3); Crispin Eurich: p. 17, 28; Eric Jukes: p. 25, 77; P. Parslow: 86(2); David Whiteway: 90(2).

Dedication:
For my loving father . . . . .

ISBN-0-87666-929-1

Distributed in the U.S. by T.F.H. Publications, Inc., 211 West Sylvania Avenue, PO Box 427, Neptune, NJ 07753; in England by T.F.H. (Gt. Britain) Ltd., 13 Nutley Lane, Reigate, Surrey; in Canada to the book store and library trade by Beaverbooks Ltd., 150 Lesmill Road, Don Mills, Ontario M38 2T5, Canada; in Canada to the pet trade by Rolf C. Hagen Ltd., 3225 Sartelon Street, Montreal 382, Quebec; in Southeast Asia by Y.W. Ong, 9 Lorong 36 Geylang, Singapore 14; in Australia and the South Pacific by Pet Imports Pty. Ltd., P.O. Box 149, Brookvale 2100, N.S.W. Australia; in South Africa by Valid Agencies, P.O. Box 51901, Randburg 2125 South Africa. Published by T.F.H. Publications, Inc., Ltd, the British Crown Colony of Hong Kong.

BREEDING
GUINEA PIGS

JENNIFER AXELROD

(Left) A silver agouti sow with her four identical offspring are all the result of pure-bred cavy matings. It is possible to predict the phenotype (physical appearance) of such pure-bred crosses. (Below) This mating pair have almost identical coloration and pattern: rust and white with a smooth coat. Nevertheless, they may not be pure-bred.

General Introduction

So you have decided to breed guinea pigs. Here is a pictorial book designed to furnish you with the facts needed to help you succeed in your venture as well as the figures of the gestation period, breeding age, breeding life and the general requirements of *Cavia porcellus,* commonly known as the guinea pig or the cavy.

In Peru, South America, cavies are known as Cuis (kwees) and exist successfully in the wild. They are also bred domestically for food and graze on grass as if they were miniature beef cattle. The Peruvians find them to be ideal for eating since they can be cheaply kept because they are vegetarians and are also very clean animals. During

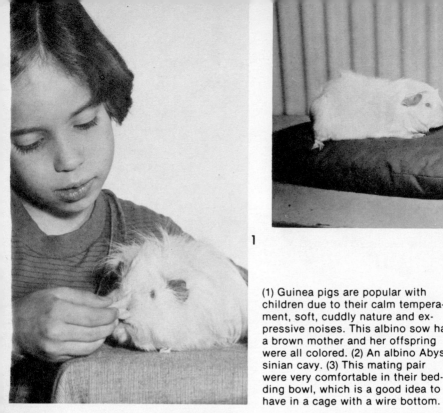

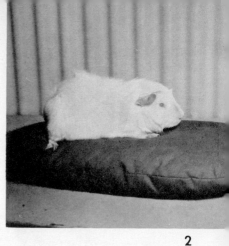

1

2

(1) Guinea pigs are popular with children due to their calm temperament, soft, cuddly nature and expressive noises. This albino sow had a brown mother and her offspring were all colored. (2) An albino Abyssinian cavy. (3) This mating pair were very comfortable in their bedding bowl, which is a good idea to have in a cage with a wire bottom.

3

These three young, charcoal black guinea pigs are one litter. During the three months following their birth they grow very rapidly and reach more than half of their adult size.

World War II, the Italians were encouraged to raise them as food animals to supplement their poor rations.

The guinea pig could have acquired part of its name from the time when the Dutch sailors took them to Guinea and then on to Europe or maybe they were sold for a guinea. How they also came to be called pigs . . . well, your guess is as good as mine.

Once upon a time I kept guinea pigs. When I undertook to write this book, I bought a trio of cavies, one boar and two sows. The albino Abyssinian turned out to be pregnant and in one month delivered her first litter. They turned out to be a gray Self, a tortoise-shell self and a tortoise-shell Abyssinian loaded with character, which I called "Harlequin". I found my childhood memories flooding back and it was good. I still have "Powderpuff", the mother, and "Harlequin."

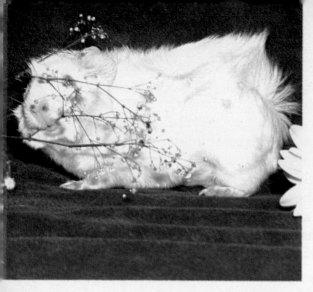

(Left) Guinea pigs will eat almost any type of vegetable matter and are easy to raise. (Below) These wild guinea pigs are found in warm climates and are raised by some people as a food source. For example, in Peru cavies are domesticated and bred for size.

Uses
Of The
Guinea Pig

The reasons for breeding the guinea pig are numerous. To start with the most obvious, they are adorable, pug-nosed, docile creatures ideal for children because they rarely bite. They are easy to keep and care for. They are also ideal companions because they squeak, purr and make bubbling noises. They seem to communicate with you and their mate. They do not cost as much as a chinchilla, an exotic bird or a fancy fish. They will also be popular as pets and thus many pet shops will want to buy your new stock. As gifts for children and older people, they are usually well received. They are hardier and easier to handle than birds like the great macaws that can break a button in their beak

with one twist of their heads. Guinea pigs are also inexpensive to maintain; their food and upkeep is not astronomical. Provided that you keep their housing facilities sanitary, they are meticulous about their cleanliness. Taking all of this into account, as well as the necessity for an essential nutritional requirement of a vitamin C-oriented diet, they should give the owner at least five years of pleasure and companionship.

If you plan to breed cavies for research or laboratory purposes, their value as experimental animals has long been established. They are used in many drug tests from aspirin to penicillin. They are also used in disease studies to determine, for example, whether or not a patient has contracted tuberculosis. If the guinea pig shows the same symptoms as the patient after inoculation then an accurate diagnosis can be made. They are also used in studies of diphtheria, cancer and effects of radiation from x-rays and atomic explosions. Guinea pigs are also used in germ free research, where the young are born by Caesarian section and live in completely sterilized containers, eat only sterilized food and breathe filtered air. Then germs are introduced and the side effects closely watched without any other strains of disease to interfere with the results. The handlers either wear plastic gloves that protrude from the plastic or stainless steel tanks and are put on "inside out" or the animals are handled with remote control manipulators. Naturally the relatively long life of the guinea pig, unlike the shorter lives that many other rodents lead, is very beneficial to these experimenters.

Guinea pigs are also used for nutrition studies. The federal and state governments in the U.S. require that the foods, cosmetics and other products maintain the quality of their ingredients at set minimum standards. Such quality controls could not possibly be employed with such stringency unless the products were first tested on animals such as the guinea pig. This small rodent is also used in testing new drugs and the biological potency of their chemical substances. Medical researchers often use the guinea pig in their experiments involving muscular dystrophy. This is because that part of the animal's histology is closely related to man's.

Intelligence studies on the guinea pig show that it rates low on the I.Q. standard scale. Their whole way of life, including feeding, exemplifies this. They are vegetarians and do not have to use speed and cunning to hunt for their food. They are gentle and timid and prefer to sit still rather than explore. They are not as curious as rats or chipmunks when they are subjected to maze studies. They fail miserably and prefer to munch at the maze or just bunch themselves at the start of the maze pattern.

Guinea pigs are especially useful in heredity studies where the geneticist can trace how traits like hair color and eye color are passed on from parents to offspring. Chemical packets called genes, which are found in every cell of the animal body, control the heredity factors. For the breeder interested in genetics, there are many specimens from which to choose. They range from the smooth self variety to those that look like Yorkshire Terriers. The Peruvian or the Sheltie variety has hair and a mane up to eight inches long and the animal cavorts around like an animated mop. This is the challenge in breeding guinea pigs. What variety do you want to specialize in and how can you select and breed the particular colors you want? One must also choose desirable physical characteristics that, for example, make the specimen an Abyssinian with ten rosettes or a crested Sheltie with one rosette like a crown on its head. Hamsters, gerbils and mice do not have this variety of breeds and coloration and, therefore, they lack the element of surprise and genetic challenge that guinea pigs provide.

There are many different breeds for the geneticist to experiment with and receive definite visual proof of his hypotheses. Human beings, by comparison, only have a

(Left) "Harlequin," a tortoise-shell and white Abyssinian, was part of the first litter of the author's albino Abyssinians. He is loaded with character and is therefore a favorite. Guinea pigs are adorable and docile creatures, ideal for children because they rarely bite. They seem to communicate with you and each other with squeaking, purring and bubbling noises. (Above) Peruvian guinea pigs grow long flowing hair. This dark tricolor Peruvian shows good frontal hair over its face.

(1) Guinea pigs grow to several pounds in weight. You can weigh your pet without too much trouble using a simple scale as seen here. Guinea pigs of this size are not uncommon. (2) Children and guinea pigs have always been a good combination. It is important, however, to teach your child the proper way to hold the animal so that it will feel comfortable and safe, and not try to squirm away.

1

2

Guinea pigs shows and auctions are more popular in Europe than they are in America. Here a girl carefully studies several Himalayan guinea pigs which are on display at a show.

few children and no geneticist can tell a person which mate to choose for procreation. With the guinea pig the researcher can arrange as many matings as he pleases. He can also choose to mate brothers with sisters and parents with children, a freedom he cannot possibly exercise with human beings. Thus he can also study various diseases which run in families. This has in turn helped us to understand how diseases and defects, such as diabetes, hemophilia and color blindness, are inherited.

Whether you breed your animals for sale in a pet shop, for your own study and enjoyment or for research activities in schools, hospitals or laboratories, this book will answer some of the questions you will have and help you cope with some of the difficulties you might encounter. This book is intended to give you a better understanding of what you are or will be dealing with when breeding guinea pigs.

17

There are many different types of guinea pig breeds with different coat textures, lengths and colors. (Left) A tortoise-shell and white Abyssinian male and an albino Abyssinian female were among the author's pets. (Below) These guinea pigs of various colors and ages seem to be happy in their rocky habitat. They should also have a soft area on which to rest.

Choosing Your Guinea Pig

When you begin to look for a breeding pair, you should note that good offspring do not come from poor parents. For parenting, the sow (female) is most important. Choose a calm sow. She must not be startled when you approach her slowly for the first time. If she appears skittish and nervous to the point of being neurotic then forget her. If she is startled when she is nursing, she could easily panic and eat her young or, at the least, trample her young while she runs around the cage in an hysterical fit. Look for signs of good health in both sexes. These include shiny eyes with no mucus around them and a glossy fur with no patches of baldness except if they appear behind the ears. When you

pick up the animal, it must not be bony and the ears should not have bites or scabs on them. Overcrowded animals may nip at each other, especially if there are two boars (males) in the same cage and a serious infection may set in. The nose should not be running and the belly should not be bloated unless you are examining a pregnant sow. If you see anything that looks like a small pimple, it could be the beginning of mange. This is an infectious disease that is very difficult to eliminate or control. The hair around the rear should not be soiled or stuck together; the animal may have a case of diarrhea. You do not want to be stuck with a sick animal.

There are many varieties of breeds and if you are going to become a selective breeder, then you may want to specialize in a particular breed. You will otherwise find yourself faced with a lot of guesswork and many physical "surprises." Selective breeding is also important if one wants to avoid the in-breeding problems that can lead to such conditions as polydactylism (an extra toe), a motley collection of colors or other unexpected things. A haphazard way of breeding does not present any challenge to the breeder. If you plan to breed your guinea pigs for research, remember that most laboratories require albino guinea pigs and some may even make special demands on the breeder for pedigree studies or for pigs that have only been exposed to a certain diet. Strict breeding controls and an understanding of genetics will help you avoid a pot-luck assortment of offspring.

At this point it would be good to indicate some of the prominent cavy color varieties. The self varieties are those that are the same color all over and have a smooth, short coat. Some of the many different colors are separated as follows:

The Self Black: These animals are truly beautiful with the black luster reaching right down to the skin. The eyes are also black.

The Self White: They can be pink-eyed or black-eyed, but their fur must be snow white and silky throughout. The feet and ears must also be white with pink skin.

The Self Cream: This variety should have ruby eyes to set off the pale creamy color of the fur coat, which ideally should be free of a lemon or yellow tinge.

The Self Beige: They should resemble a beige cloth or the color of raw silk and have ears and feet to match. This breed has a body shape that is usually longer than the other self breeds. The eyes are pink.

The Self Golden: They should have the antiqued appearance of an old gold coin. The eyes are pink.

The Self Red: The coat should be a rich mahogany color with a fiery light to it. The youngsters are born with a coat that changes from light to dark and then back again. The eyes are ruby red.

The Self Chocolate: They have very soft coats and their skin is lighter than their hair so that the area around the eye appears pinkish. The nose looks like it's been dipped into strawberry-flavored chocolate. The eyes are red.

The Agouti: This is similar to the guinea pig's wild color in South America. The tip and base of each hair is black with a bar of color in the middle which can be either cinnamon, gold or silver depending on the type. The belly is usually a basic color of either a rich gold, a pale silver-platinum or a reddish-brown cinnamon.

The Dutch Variety: This is a real challenge to the breeder because of the particular bands of clearly defined color areas that are needed for the Dutch variety to be classified as this breed. It demands that the markings on the cheeks, ears and hindquarters are one basic color. The underlying background color forms a band around the middle and a stripe down the face.

Tortoise-Shell and White Mix: An excellent specimen should have between six and ten black, red and white

1

2

Here are several color varieties of smooth-haired guinea pigs. (1 & 2) Tortoise-shell and white. (3) Self-beige. Note the show of curiosity. (4) These five guinea pigs all have Dutch markings. From left to right: Golden agouti, red, black, chocolate and silver agouti.

3

4

square patches. They should ideally be of equal size and run alternately down each side of the body. This kind is the most difficult and the most challenging to breed, and a perfect specimen challenges even the most zealous genetically-minded breeders.

The Abyssinian

There should be four rosettes around and across the middle part of the body called the saddle. These swirls of hair should run around the back in an arc that rises to a peak of hair on the rump. The body should ideally have ten rosettes with pronounced ridges that make the rosettes look good and give them depth. When you choose a stud in this breed, care should be taken to ensure that your final choice is the one with clearly defined ridges. The harsher coat is the better one. The colors range from brindle with the tawny and black hairs all swirled into each other to the tortoise-shell with patches of red and black. The general roan has a basic color of black, red, gray or brown with muted, lightened mixtures of white hairs. The strawberry roan, for example, has a mixture of red and white while the tortoise-shell roan has red, black and white markings. The self Abyssinian guinea pigs can be any color provided that they are uniformly one color all over their body with no flecks of another color in the fur. When you buy a pair or trio, the male should have the choicest color and form and be as near to the standard as possible.

The Himalayan

This breed is easier to describe in terms of a comparison with a Siamese cat. The markings are identical. The extremities are dark, being either black or brown, and the rest of the body is creamy white. The young, however, are not defined until they are five to six months old.

24

Note the rosettes on the saddle of this tortoise-shell and white Abyssinian.

LONG-HAIRED BREEDS

The Peruvian

This is a very long-haired breed and the adults have hair as long as eight inches. When mating, they must have the hair shaved around their genitals to facilitate the process. These guinea pigs look like animated mops and it is fun to guess which side is which without peering under the hair to find a backside or two beady eyes. When they are born, they have two rosettes on the rump and short hair which grows towards the ears. During the summer months, if you are not using your animal for show purposes, the hair should be cut to prevent heat exhaustion or rolled in wrappers of paper or cloth and fastened with an elastic band. The side hair is also put into wrappers as soon as the hair grows long enough. If you decide to keep these long-haired breeds, always see that they are provided with hay or dried alfalfa on which to chew or they will begin to chomp on their own or their mate's manes out of boredom.

(1) A mating pair of Himalayan cavies. (2) An albino Abyssinian sow. (3) A tricolor Peruvian boar. (4) A tortoise-shell and white Abyssinian.

1

2

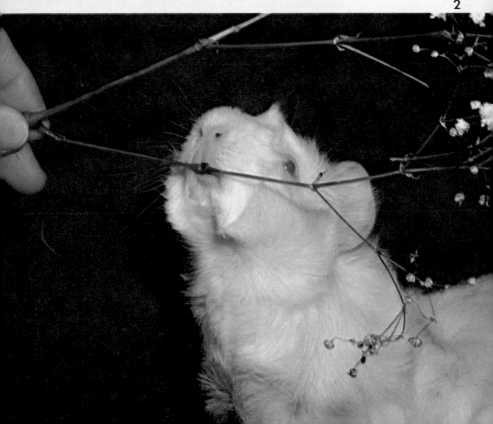

3

4

The Sheltie

This is a new breed that is very similar to the Peruvian except for one radical difference: the hair on the head sweeps back in one long mane leaving the face exposed so that it looks like a miniature Pekingese dog. They need only one wrapper to keep the coat in order. All color mixings are acceptable.

The Crested Sheltie

This looks like the Sheltie but has a rosette of hair which looks like a little crown on the top of its head. In America, they are accepted with the crest being a different color from the rest of the body while in Britain, the crest can be the same color or a totally different color from the rest of the body.

The above is just a quick summary of the different breeds. You may want to refer to the American Breeder's Club for more specialized information. Their present addresses are as follows:

The American Rabbit and Cavy Breeders Association
2401 E. Oakland Ave.
Bloomington, IL 61701

The American Cavy Breeders Association
Gen. Sec'y Treasurer
6560 Upham Street
Arvada, CO 80003

In England all breeds have specialized clubs representing them. For example, the self breeds have the English Self Breed Club. The National Cavy Club, known as the N.C.C., is recognized as the main cavy club in Great Britain.

(Left) A little girl watches the guinea pigs at a British cavy show.

(1) A golden-silver agouti. (2) A Sheltie is a new breed which is very similar in appearance to the Peruvian. In the Sheltie the hair on the head sweeps back in one long mane leaving the face exposed. (3 & 4) Wrapping a Sheltie's coat is necessary to keep the animal's hair in good order.

1

2

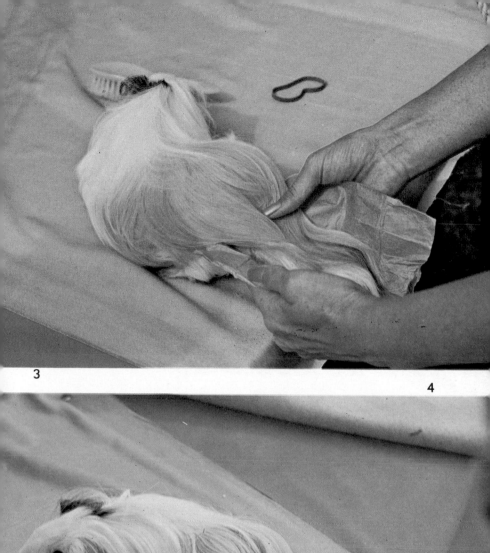

(Left) A guinea pig's housing is one of the most important elements in its overall care. Although wood may be used, it is important that it be thick enough so that the animal cannot chew through it. Here a guinea pig can be seen paring down his teeth. (Below) Outdoor cages are only possible in warm climates. They can be used to house large numbers of animals, but care should be taken to keep the guinea pigs free of bugs.

Housing

To begin with we will start this section with the pair you have chosen. Later in the chapter we will move onto a discussion of breeding on a large scale for profit.

For the beginner I recommend the use of an all-glass aquarium. It is constructed glass to glass and does not have metal trimmings at the sides. You can then watch the pair at close range. This housing facility has the added advantage of shielding its inhabitants from drafts that can cause them to get colds and possibly pneumonia as complications set in. Also, as the guinea pig is no Olympic gymnast, it is not necessary to keep a wire cover on top of the cage unless you have dogs or cats that could injure your pets. Choose a

large aquarium, like a twenty gallon aquarium for a pair and a thirty gallon one for a trio. Guinea pigs like to run around and chase each other especially when they are making preliminary overtures before mating.

In this case the boar makes a grand show of masculinity. The added space also gives the female a chance to get out of his clutches if she is not too keen to conform to his desires. It is miserable to spend one's entire existence confined between four pieces of glass or wood which encompass too small a space.

Another kind of housing is the wire cages. Like the aquaria, you can find these in pet shops. They are like bird cages with wire floors and a tray underneath that can be removed and cleaned. This tray can be sterilized chemically or with heat. The advantage of these cages is that the animals are always kept clean and dry with the droppings and urine falling to the cleaning tray. This saves on the expense of bedding materials as newsprint can be used as an absorbing base. When the sow is littering, the wire cage has an added advantage in that you do not have to disturb the animals when cleaning.

These cages, however, have to be placed in sheltered areas and kept at temperatures higher than 65°F. In addition, the babies have the added danger of getting their little feet caught in the wire openings and this might result in permanent physical damage.

For commercial breeding, some breeders prefer to use hutches stacked on top of each other. In this way they can supervise their entire community in an apartment-like concentrated block. These can be made of softwood or any other suitable, cheap material or timber that will not bend or warp. The framework is made up of substantial pieces of wood 2″ by 1″ in thickness. Masonite hardwood is better than ordinary wood because the sides can be cut in one piece and no feces or dirt can become wedged in between the joints. The depth of the hutch should be at least one foot and the height at least 18″. The length of the housing space depends entirely on you and your breeding community and how you want to utilize your breeding space. Each "floor" is occupied with one boar and six sows. Some breeders prefer to keep one boar with twelve sows, but this is overcrowding the space. It is unlikely that the boar may try to harm the litter as other sows will divert his interests. The sows, however, may panic from a sudden noise that startles them or they may rampage during feeding time and trample a newly born litter. I prefer the method of separating the pregnant sow from the rest of the litter before she is due, but this involves more housing space and generally more upkeep and care.

In laboratories, where the cleanliness of the animals' housing must be kept under stringent control, the guinea pigs are kept in stainless steel cages. These cages are my second choice after aquariums because they can be fully sterilized with antiseptic in a tub. These cages are also ideal because unlike plastic cages they resist corrosion, are impervious to many chemicals, are strong and are resistant to gnawing.

Stainless steel cages can sometimes be purchased from pet shops or they can be ordered and made to your specifications by a stainless steel or metal factory in your area. Although they are initially expensive, they are a good investment because they can be easily maintained in good condition for a long time and they can be sold for a good price after they have been used.

To summarize there are two kinds of designs that can be made to specification, built or improvised. These are the "shoe box" and "front opening" cages. The former would be a design like the aquarium and the latter would be like the hutches with hinged doors. The bottoms of the front opening cages are usually fitted with sliding floor trays to facilitate the removal of droppings. These kinds of cages should be kept on metal stands in a sheltered area with no drafts but where adequate ventilation can occur. The best material for these stands is steel.

Animals often use their personal smell for territory marking and the wild running movements guinea pigs perform when they are first put into a cage is their way of marking their territory. If there is some scent of the cage's former inhabitants or even if a water bottle from another pig's cage is used, the new guinea pigs will take some time before they settle down. Do not worry. The guinea pigs will soon become accustomed to whatever cage you provide for them.

TYPES OF BEDDING

Sawdust is useless as it can contain poisonous phenolic substances (caustic poisonous acidic compounds present in wood tar) that can contaminate your animals. It also tends to clot when it becomes wet and it is bad for nesting material as it could stick to the young guinea pigs' eyes and partially blind them.

Peat moss litter is obtainable from fodder merchants and this can be just as bad as sawdust as it has a high acid content and it can be dusty.

Straw works very well, but because the guinea pigs chew it as food, it must be constantly renewed and kept fresh. Be sure that it is dry and not green in color. There must not be too much straw present when there are young about as they can get lost in it, get trampled by the adults or run against one protruding straw and poke out their eyes.

Flax plant fiber is a very good absorbent.

Ground corncob is good because it keeps the smells down to a minimum. It is also absorbent and will not injure the inhabitants. It is also good for litters as the guinea pig sow can dig up a temporary "nest" in the corn cobs for her little nursery.

Hardwood chips are also good, but they can cause the sipper tube from the water bottle to clog.

Dust free shavings, especially cedar chips, are the best

material for bedding because they not only are absorbent but they also keep small mites and lice away.

Newspaper is your last resort and I mean your last resort.

Whichever bedding material you decide to use, always ensure that the material is kept clean and dry. I would recommend that you change the bedding twice a week or more, especially if you keep your pet in your bedroom or living room where the animal's contentment as well as yours is at stake.

After the bedding material is placed in the cage, you can proceed to furnish your guinea pig with other necessary items. See that all food is in a raised dish above the litter and that the opening of the receptacle is not too wide. Guinea pigs love to sit in their food dishes and defecate. The water bottle should be hung from the side of the cage and should be made of plastic and stainless steel with a stainless steel ball bearing tip to impede the flow of water back into the bottle. The ball bearing should be made of stainless steel rather than plastic because the guinea pig constantly chews the spout. A plastic ball bearing tends to get stuck in the middle of the spout and the water constantly drips out into the cage. A salt block should also be provided for your guinea pig. This can be hung from the top of the cage with a wire.

The guinea pig, like humans and other mammals, needs to have a constant supply of vitamin C in its diet to prevent scurvy. No other rodent has the same problem. Without vitamin C the gums start to swell and bleed, and the bones and teeth can become permanently damaged. Sailors of the 17th and 18th centuries were often known to show manifestations of this deficiency when they were unable to obtain fresh greens or produce and had to eat salted meat. Garden stations were established at different ports and this problem was eliminated. Your guinea pig can get this nutritional requirement from greens, tomatoes and most especially from a tonic with a measured dosage of essential vitamins that can be added to the drinking water. Thus you will no longer have to worry whether or not your pet is getting the required amount of vitamins.

SUMMARY OF USEFUL DATA ON THE GUINEA PIG

- The lifespan of the guinea pig is six years.
- The minimum breeding age for the boar is ten to fourteen weeks and for the sow eleven to sixteen weeks.
- I would suggest mating one boar to every four females although many breeders like to put one boar to twelve sows.
- The gestation time is sixty-two to seventy-four days.
- The average litter size is two to four young.
- The weaning age is fourteen to eighteen days.
- The breeding life for the sow and boar is four years.
- The heart beat is 250 beats a minute.
- The daily food consumption is twenty to thirty grams (1 ounce) for a guinea pig weighing three hundred grams. (10 ounces).
- The daily water consumption is eighty-five milliliters (one tenth of a quart).
- The daily urinary rate is twenty to twenty-five milliliters (one tenth of a cup).
- The room temperature should preferably remain between 75°—80°F., the humidity should not go higher than 55-65 percent and they should not be exposed to direct sunlight. In the winter the guinea pig can tolerate a temperature of about 65°F.

  Small mammal heaters are sold in pet shops, but there is the possibility that the guinea pigs will chew through the wires and electrocute themselves. There would be no point in installing one on top of the aquarium or housing area because heat rises.
- Guinea pigs must have a special diet and a source of vitamin C from greens or a vitamin supplement.

- The guinea pig is covered with a coat of hair that enables it to keep warm when there are extremes in temperature from a normal temperature to a colder one. Guinea pigs cannot perspire as well as the human body can because of their hair covering, so they adapt badly to changes from a normal temperature to a rise in heat. They can die easily from heat exhaustion.

HOUSING FOR COMMERCIAL BREEDERS

If you have decided to expand your small facilities into one huge breeding area on a full time basis purely with the intentions of making money, then the following details should be noted.

First, check with your local health board and observe all the zoning and health requirements.

Second, choose the space you want to convert and divide it into smaller areas. I suggest the following:

- A space should be set aside for the incoming animals, food, bedding and other new supplies.
- There should be the actual area for housing the animals and a separate area for the pregnant sows.
- You can divide these housing facilities into different areas for the different breeds so that you will not become confused.
- There should be isolation rooms for the incoming guinea pig stock until you have established whether or not they have any infections.
- There should be a storage area above the ground that is cool and dry where no other animals (like dogs or cats) can get to it.
- There should be a cleanup area where you can wash cages, water bottles, racks and any other equipment.
- There must also be a waste disposal space that is completely set apart from the food or housing area.
- If you plan to employ workers, rest rooms and dress-

ing facilities and maybe a shower should be made available.

- An administrative space should be planned so that you can conduct your business efficiently.
- The entire space must be disinfected before the animals arrive and all openings should be screened to prevent the entry of any flying insects. The floors should be of a substance that can easily be disinfected and mopped; they should be swept every day and mopped with disinfectant twice a week.
- Workers should report injuries immediately and prompt medical action should be taken to prevent infection from any bites or injuries.
- There should be no smoking, drinking or eating in the animal rooms. All soiled litter and debris should be disposed of immediately either by incineration or dumping (preferably the former if you have the facilities).
- All clothing worn in the animal room should be clean and freshly laundered and all garments soiled by the animals should be removed and disinfected as soon as possible.
- A constant temperature between 68°-78°F. is ideal and the humidity should be between 55-65 percent.
- Workers should wash their hands after handling any animals and after cleaning each cage so no possible cross infection occurs.

PACKING AND SHIPPING

There are pasteboard cartons designed especially for packing and shipping guinea pigs. They are used only once and then discarded. They have a protective covering on the inside and are lined with mesh to prevent escape and provide adequate ventilation. Abundant bedding is placed in the pasteboard cartons to protect the animals in transit as well as afford them some privacy if they want to hide. A small amount of food is placed in the container and a raw carrot or an apple placed with it for moisture. If they are transported by vans, adequate ventilation should be provided and the temperature kept as constant as possible. Animals are usually sold by weight, but sometimes researchers need certain characteristics. For example, only old pigs would be needed for geriatric studies. Any such condition will reflect on the selling price. Some researchers may even want the animals specifically raised in the dark for a specified time; this is very inconvenient so the selling price would be much higher than normal.

(1) An all glass aquarium (with a wire-mesh lid) is recommended by the author as it is comfortable for the animal, is easily kept warm, and keeps the litter from falling out of the housing and causing a mess. It must, however, be cleaned regularly. (2) A wire cage is easy to keep clean but it is difficult to keep warm and is less comfortable for the animal than an all glass aquarium. (3) Year-round outdoor housing is only possible in warm climates. Care must be taken to keep cage and animals free of harmful lice, ticks, and other bugs. Also, a good enclosure is necessary to keep snakes and harmful rodents out of the cage.

1

2

3

(Left) It is important to know how to properly hold your guinea pig. (Below) All guinea pigs should have a salt block in their cages as their food may not supply enough salt. The animal will pick at the block when it has the need.

Feeding
And
General
Care

Keep records of all animal inventory on the cage as well as in the main office. As I have mentioned before, stainless steel housing and food containers are the best, but you usually will have to special order these from you pet shop or a local factory. The food containers should be able to hang from the top of the cage or be suspended from the sides and they should be able to hold a three days' supply of food without being contaminated. Materials that chip, like enamel, should never be used as food containers because such materials may become mixed with the rest of the food. Remember that guinea pigs gnaw at things and this will no doubt include the enamel dish.

(1) It is a good idea to keep a carrying or travelling box handy, in case it is necessary to move your guinea pig. (2) A proper balance of vitamins, especially vitamin C, is essential for your animal's health.

One of the most important things to remember about your guinea pig's nutritional needs is that this animal must have a daily supply of vitamin C. This can be provided in the form of a liquid supplement that is dropped into the drinking water from an eyedropper. Liquid supplements, with directions for their use, can be obtained from your local pet shop. This supplement can also be added to the food, but I prefer to add it to the water because I know then that the animals will definitely be receiving the proper requirements and that they cannot defecate in their water bottle.

Guinea pig pellets can be obtained from any pet shop, but when you buy vast quantities of them, ensure that they are fresh and that they do not have any worms or maggots in them. Store them in airtight containers. After six weeks the vitamin C content is lost through aging and after this the pellets should not be relied on for this nutritional requirement.

44

This smooth-coated cream guinea pig is very comfortable on hay.

Rabbit pellets are unsuitable for feeding because they have no vitamin C formula added to the content and the fiber in these pellets is too high.

It is far easier to purchase commercial food than try to formulate a diet yourself because each locality will have varieties of foods deficient in some essential nutriments. The differences in nutritional content result from the soil in which the foods have been grown, the length of time they have been stored and so on.

Greens should be fed to your animals if you do not provide the vitamin C supplement in the drinking water. They should, however, be fresh and something you yourself would not hesitate to eat. If the greens are old or soiled, your animal could get diarrhea.

Fresh kale and cabbage as well as lettuce are good.

Other green foods include celery tops, lawn clippings, broccoli, apples and sprouted oats. When all is said and done, however, it is easy and no problem to feed them the supplement and occasionally give them greens to sink their teeth into. This also cuts down on the unpleasant smell that results after feeding them greens.

They will enjoy gnawing dried alfalfa which can be pur-

1

2

3

(1) Cleaning the cage drop tray. (2) Washing the tray with soap and water. (3) Litter is important for comfort and warmth, and as an absorbent base. Chlorophyll litter or cedar chips will also help keep insects away from your animals. (4) An occasional treat is always welcome by your animal. (5) Most guinea pigs enjoy alfalfa.

4

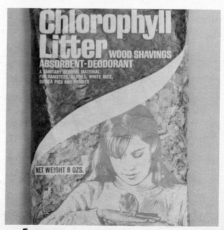

5

chased from a pet shop. This gnawing will keep their teeth from growing to a length which would not allow them to close their mouths. Alfalfa is good also because it is high in vitamins, calcium and vitamin A.

Some breeders feed their animals oats and hay, but since these high carbohydrate foodstuffs can be detrimental to the health of your animals if used for an extended period of time, you must not depend solely on them for your pet's nutritional requirements. Lucern hay is high in vitamins, calcium and vitamin A. For vitamin C good meadow hay will suffice provided that it has not been stored for a long time. It should be greenish to light yellow-brown in color and sweet-smelling. Hay with a moldy appearance should be discarded.

Guinea pigs also need a salt block which they will lick periodically and this should be hung from the top of the cage or on the side of the aquarium away from where they can urinate on it.

Any cardboard tubes, like those from paper towels and bathroom tissue, are very good for guinea pigs to chew and play with and these should be given to them on a regular basis, especially if they are not supplied with greens on which to gnaw and pare their teeth. This will help to prevent the cavies from barbering each other which can wreak great destruction on your show animals' coats. In some cases the young are stripped of all their covering. Hair loss over the entire body is probably due to a vitamin or dietary deficiency.

You will probably find yourself humoring your pet's appetite to some extent. I have found, for example, that some of my guinea pigs thoroughly enjoy lettuce while others shy away from it. I also occasionally like to feed my pigs vitamin enriched cereals soaked in milk, particularly when the females are lactating and nursing. Occasionally providing your pet's favorite foods would obviously not apply to an entire colony of the animals.

(Left) A black Abyssinian male pursues an albino Abyssinian female in the hope of mating her. (Below) Three Dutch-marked guinea pigs sitting near their awards. Careful breeding can yield champion animals like these. Cavy societies often arrange shows for competitive purposes.

Breeding

HANDLING

Guinea pigs should be lifted gently with both hands and supported from under their body and most especially by the rear end. All of the guinea pig's bulk is concentrated there and if you pick up your animal from the top without giving it the necessary support, then it could twist and injure itself internally. If you should drop the animal, this could prove fatal as it is likely to land head first or injure its spine. If you can see that the animal is in pain and is staggering around or making convulsive movements, it is best to "put it down" or to chloroform it. Sometimes a spinal injury is undetected until the female is ready to give birth;

then all the complications set in and the animal as well as the young die in the process. I must stress at this stage that the more you handle your animal the better and as soon as the babies are old enough (about a week old), then they too should be gently handled. This is particularly important if you want to sell your stock to a pet shop. They must be hand tame and respond to human handling. It is very important that you break them in gently. I own a female guinea pig that is quite neurotic from bad handling during infancy. Reward them with tidbits every time you "play" with them and they will learn to trust you and respond to you demonstratively with "kwees" sounds and great enthusiastic high-pitched squeeks whenever they want food or want to attract your attention.

Pregnant sows should not be handled, especially when they are in the advanced stages of pregnancy or you may damage the young. If she is your personal pet, very careful handling is needed and you can stroke her while she is in her cage.

As far as bathing is concerned, it is not necessary to bathe your guinea pig unless it needs it. For example, when it has had a bad case of diarrhea, if it was dirty when you purchased it from the pet shop, if you want to show it or if your particular animal is one of the long-haired breeds like the Peruvians or the Shelties, a bath will obviously improve the looks of your pet. Fill a container with lukewarm water and gently lower the animal's hindlegs into it; wet the rest of the body gradually so you do not startle it. With a mild shampoo, lather the animal and then rinse it in fresh clean water. Rub it with a dry towel until it is towel dry. You could use a hairdryer set at low speed and at a moderate heat; but if it is not a cold day, it would be better to place the animal back in its hutch with fresh litter and out of the way of drafts and it will dry itself. If you keep the litter clean at all times, bathing should not be necessary, for, like a cat, a guinea pig will clean itself continually.

The sexing of your animal must be handled with care so as not to hurt it. Press gently in the area between the legs and the abdomen. If the cavy is a boar (male), a small penis will protrude like a telescope. If the animal is a sow (female), nothing will happen.

SEXING

The way to sex a guinea pig is to lie it gently against your body resting in the crook of your arm and gently press the area between the legs in the abdomen. If the pig is a boar, a small penis will protrude like a telescope and if it is a sow, nothing will happen. Do not exert any heavy pressure to do this and do not do this with young guinea pigs as this area may not yet be fully developed and you may permanently damage your breeding chances and your guinea pig in the bargain. You can sex your animal after three to four weeks.

BREEDING METHODS

The method for breeding guinea pigs is something about which some experts disagree. The controversy centers around the issue of *monogamous or pair breeding* as opposed to *polygamous or colony breeding*. With the first form, the sow and boar remain together only until the litter is born and with the second form the male is left continuously with the females.

51

The advantage of leaving the male with the females even during the birth is that the female can almost immediately be made pregnant by the boar after the delivery. This is called post partum mating. Thus maximum productivity can be maintained. The disadvantage of this system is that the boar may injure the babies or if a sudden noise startles the rest of the colony he and the other females may run hysterically around the housing space and injure the new-born litter. Some of the young may even be trampled to death. It also becomes difficult if not impossible to determine the breeding abilities of a particular female when you have four others littering in the same area.

Some breeders transfer the pregnant sow to another cage or housing unit so she can devote her attention entirely to her young. In this way, clear accurate records can be kept of the litter and the sow's breeding performance and if you are working by the selective breeding method, then this is absolutely essential. This method, however, also has its disadvantages because more cages are needed, as well as the space in which to keep them, and more manpower is necessary to attend to the basic needs and hygiene of the animals.

The third method is to remove the guinea pig female to another housing area and wait for her to have her litter. You then record the details of the delivery and replace her and the two week old litter back with the main herd and most especially with the boar for further matings to take place. This method enables a high percentage of post partum matings to take place and results in a high level of productivity over a period of eighteen months. One major problem with this method is that a lactating female will nurse any young that approach her. If the young from another litter come to her, she will quite willingly feed them and thus be drained of her milk so that when she gives birth to her litter, there is not enough.

There are three types of breeding: crossbreeding, line breeding and inbreeding.

With the *crossbreeding* method it is difficult to predict what the outcome will be. It can be used purely as an experimental method that develops new strains. Mendel proved that this could increase the vigor of the breed, but it is known to also produce undesirable variations and it may endow the offspring with traits that are unwanted. Be sure to choose a pair with the best qualities.

Line breeding involves mating the descendants back to a desirable ancestor like some stud in the colony or a sow that has proven her mothering abilities. If the mating is between distant relatives, there is no problem of degeneration. This type of breeding method results in successful improvements in size, color or shape and can produce fine show animals.

Inbreeding is intensive line breeding which can fix desirable or undesirable characteristics in the strain. It may also lead to a general weakening and degeneration of the strain. It is obviously a method that must not be applied for periods of extended duration. If you use this method, choose the best of the litter for breeding. Weaning the males and the females separately eliminates the guesswork and enables you to select good breeding stock.

Whichever method you choose to use, remember that the animals used from the outset for breeding should be purchased from the best possible source. Only the best specimens should be kept for breeding purposes and used to improve the stock.

THE POST PARTUM PHENOMENON

This is the ability of the female guinea pig to become pregnant in the presence of a boar a few hours after giving birth to a litter. There is a good chance that another pregnancy will be well advanced by the time her original litter is reared. Thus a healthy sow should be capable of producing five litters in one year. The young are healthy and the sows do not suffer any ill effects from this form of intensive breeding.

FACTS TO REMEMBER WHEN BREEDING

Breed systematically and keep detailed records.

Select good breeding stock and cull poor producers.

Breed more females than you need to compensate for any losses, misses and destroyed litters.

When you breed you must take the female to the male and not the other way around or she may reject him and fight with him. They can become quite violent, biting and nipping each other's ears and kicking each other. Serious fighting must be stopped immediately. If they seem amiable, leave them together on a trial basis, especially if this is their first mating.

The most fertile matings occur when the female is eighty to eighty-five days old. In females mated after this period, the female's pelvic points fuse. This is dangerous because by this time the pelvis is narrowed around the birth canal and labor can be difficult. It may even prevent the young from being born alive and well.

It is good to place the boar with no more than four females because if an infection sets in the entire colony will be threatened and the incidence for this happening with overcrowding is very common. It also makes smaller animals compete for food and they can be lost to the breeder.

The estrus cycle starts at sixty-eight days of age and repeats itself every sixteen to nineteen days. The heat cycle is polyestrous which means that they have cycles all year round. At this time she is receptive to the male. When the male fertilizes her, the cycle will be interrupted while the young are developing within her. This lasts for sixty to seventy days and is called the gestation period. Within six to eight hours following the birth, she is ready to be mated again because her estrus cycle reoccurs. Do not wait too long between litterings because you want to maintain maximum productivity and the young should be born while the sow is still in her prime.

The first possible litter is at twenty weeks. The average litter size is three, but it can range from two to nine. The birth weight is about two and a half to three ounces and the baby will be eating solids by the time it is two to three days old.

If the young are unsatisfactory and have a poor physical appearance, check the male's report card so you can keep tabs on his future reproductive activities and the results of the offspring of the other sows this particular stud served.

After weaning separate the females and the males as this will eliminate the guesswork when you decide to breed them.

According to specialists the breeding life of the male is five years and the female's is four to five years.

INFERTILITY

This can be caused by a number of factors. One major reason for this condition may be a poor diet and a lack of essential vitamins, especially vitamin C. Another possible dietary factor may be malnutrition. Insufficient water will cause the animals to automatically eat less since there would be nothing to aid in the digestion of dry food pellets. This can cause the animals to eat nothing at all or at least it could cause constipation. If constipation is not relieved it can be fatal, with initial bleeding around the rectal area and complications in pregnancy.

Overheating, shortened daylight hours, inadequate lighting, overpopulation and bad living conditions can also result in infertility. Noise can frighten lactating females and they can either neglect their young or dry up. Overcrowding also slows the growth rate and can spread diseases among the young that have a low resistance. All these factors influence the fertility or the mortality rate of the breeding guinea pig.

KEEPING RECORDS

It is easy to identify an animal if it has some coloration that distinguishes it from all the rest of the colony, but it becomes hellishly difficult to do this when they are all albino or tortoise-shell or one of the self varieties. In this case it is no longer effective only to keep records; you must find some other way to mark the animals to facilitate the record keeping routine in the animal colony. It is necessary to keep records as well as to mark the individual animals. You should choose a method that you like and stick with it rather than experiment with all of the ones suggested below. This will avoid confusion. Obviously an animal that has a peculiar marking, hair length or hair texture does not need any physical disfigurement; it only needs a record card.

An Example of a Typical Record Card

SPECIES	STRAIN	SEX	NUMBER
CAGE NUMBER	RACK NUMBER		DATE BORN
PARENTS: MALE		FEMALE	

DATE MATED MATED WITH YOUNG BORN DATE NO. RAISED

DISPOSITIONS	REMARKS

Methods of marking guinea pigs are as follows:

Dyeing or shaving the fur. This is not a permanent fixture and can only be used for short term identification. The hair either grows back or is shed.

Leg bands on the hind legs. This is done much as one would band a bird.

Ear marking studs. These studs are made of aluminum and applied close to the head with the studs numbered or lettered in a predetermined code. The studs are inserted into the guinea pig's ear like a woman's pierced earring. A week or two later the ear should be inspected and bathed with a mild antiseptic to prevent infection.

Notches and punches. These are done by the same gadget that is used for the ear marking studs. Below is an ear marking code made up of both notches and punches although with the leafy ear of the guinea pig it is difficult to see the notches. The punches are clear and defined. You can be inventive and devise your own codes using this as a "kick off" to inspire you.

LEFT	FOR EXAMPLE		RIGHT	24	WILL BE	
10	20	30	40	1	2	3	4

Tattooing is not suggested because it requires general anesthesia. Unless you are an expert in this field, you could kill your animals or physically injure them with the needles.

The decision about which method to use is up to you and depends on what purposes you have for breeding. If you wish to show your animals, then obviously the record keeping will have to suffice. If it is for a pet shop sale, none of the above permanent markings will be acceptable. The only time you could freely use permanent "fixtures" would be in laboratories or for research purposes when a certain code would define a particular diet, age group or animal if, for example, your entire stock was albino.

It is not a necessity to mark your own personal pets.

Accurately kept records and defined codes must accompany any permanent, physical markings.

THE BIRTH PROCESS

Because guinea pigs are very secretive and private about this process, you will see the birth only if you are lucky. You will more likely wake up one morning and see that she has delivered overnight. If you are lucky enough to be there, this is what your will see. First you will notice that she is very still and huddles up in a corner: then strong ripples appear down the side of her belly. A while later a package wrapped in a shiny bag comes out of her rear end. She will bite this open, strip it off and lick the newly emerged baby clean. Then a small object which looks like raw liver comes out; this was the baby's lifeline with all the food materials and oxygen that the guinea pig needed for growth while it was within the sow's womb. Although the sow is a vegetarian, she will gobble the placenta. Then she will care for the miniature copies of herself. Do not interfere with this process in any way. She is more than capable and you will just confuse her, upset her and make the process very difficult. If anything should happen to her, another female will willingly suckle the orphans, providing the new female is lactating.

Young guinea pigs are self-sufficient and can eat solid food within a day of their being born. These clown-like looking animals are in fact the rodent mammalian whizz kid with all the powers of an adult, fully furred, open-eyed and mobile. They look like one giant guinea pig head with four feet attached.

If the litter is scattered when they are born leave them alone even if they appear dead. She will collect them and gather them to her when she wants to nurse them.

WHELPING AND WEANING

The baby guinea pig should weigh two and a half to four ounces at birth and any babies weighing less than two ounces have only a slim chance of surviving. The males are usually heavier than the females and the smaller the number of young in a litter, the heavier they are and the more chance they have of a successful survival. The female or sow only has two mammary glands and more than three young cannot receive adequate nourishment. You can supplement their diet in this instance by feeding the young diluted evaporated milk or milk for human babies that you can purchase in the supermarkets. Feed them with a water bottle with a stainless steel sipper tube every two to three hours for the first week. You can also keep soaked pellets and chopped cabbage nearby in the housing space in case they want to eat it. Guinea pig babies are born very well developed with a complete coat, a full set of teeth and open eyes. Other rodent babies, such as rats, are born blind, pink, naked and incredibly helpless.

The guinea pig baby develops at a fantastic rate gaining about one sixth of an ounce per day for the first two months. Records of the litter size and the growth and condition of the babies should be rigorously kept with notes made on general health, the size and frequency of the litters, the mothering ability of the sow and whether or not she has enough milk to feed her offspring, the tameness of the young and the mother, the ease of handling (this is providing that you handle her gently and care for her well), the size of the babies and their growth rate. Many of these qualities are inherited and many are a result of the environment, eating habits and diet of the colony. You should be able to differentiate between these qualities.

The lactating sow should be provided with more protein content than normal. Supply her with milk or soak the food pellets in milk because it eliminates nursing discomfort. If she does not have enough milk with which to feed the young, they will suck harder. A quiet sow will jump from the nest and lick her young while a nervous one will bite at the young in a frenzy; the latter, however, is very rare. Do not handle her while she is mothering and keep strong odors, such as those made by cooking or smoking, away from her.

Even though the babies are self-sufficient three days after the birth and are eating solid foods, the weaning period lasts for two to three weeks during which time you should separate the litter by placing the males in one cage and the females in another to maintain a strict control of the breeding. Only the litters of the best mother should be kept as breeders and the others should be sold to pet shops or other organizations. When you are ready to breed the guinea pigs, they should be inspected for signs of general good health and the qualities that you want to inbreed. After this inspection separate them into paired monogamous couples or into polygamous colonies. As the offspring of young breeding couples are more healthy and vigorous than the older breeding animals, it is important to discard old sows and boars in preference to the younger animals.

The mating sequence between a black male and albino female begins with (1) the male trying to mount the female from the wrong end (this frequently happens), (2) the male cornering the female and attempting to mount, (3) the male smelling the female, and (4) a successful mounting and mating.

4

(Left) When you keep or bring your guinea pig outdoors, it is a good idea to spray the animal in order to prevent it from getting fleas or ticks. (Below) A veterinarian examines a guinea pig.

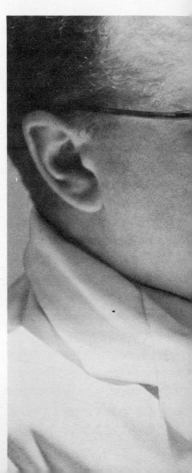

Ailments And Cures

Intestinal Infections

1) Salmonellosis

The diet which includes moldy foodstuffs or frosted or rotting greenstuffs may bring on this disease. Visable symptoms include an arched back, wasting and diarrhea.

2) Edema disease

This is a swelling of the abdomen or edema in the peritoneum. The diet again is at fault. It may have contained a toxic substance or may have been formulated incorrectly. This, however, is unlikely if you purchased it from a pet shop. Visible symptoms include excessive thirst and excessive swelling in the abdominal region. For both of the above ailments consult a veterinarian.

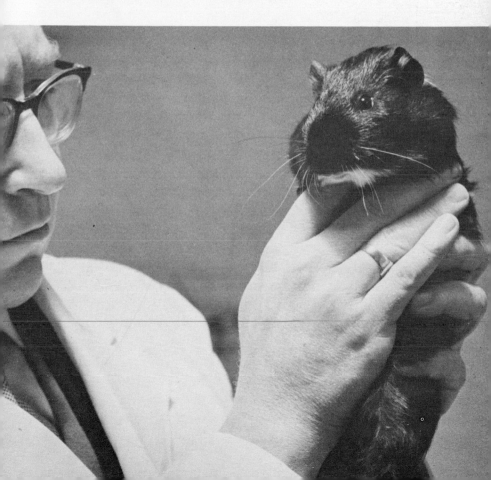

Guinea Pig Paralysis

The animal may appear hunched over and unable to raise its head. Other symptoms include high temperature, loss in weight with gradual muscular weakness and paralysis in the hind legs. This can be caused by an uncommon virus or by the animal being confined in a cramped area. A change in the living space of the animal will cure this mild temporary form of paralysis. If the paralysis is more serious, lack of vitamin D or a spinal injury may be the cause. If it is the latter, the kindest thing to do would be to destroy the animal by euthanasia. You can ask your veterinarian to take care of this for you.

If a pregnant female has a *spinal injury* but shows no visible signs of it, she could die during childbirth. Spinal injuries can be caused by manhandling a pregnant female, dropping the animal or picking it up incorrectly.

Vitamin C Deficiency

Deficiency of vitamin C can cause scurvy. The gums start to swell and bleed. A diet which includes fresh greens or a vitamin supplement added to the daily water supply will prevent the deficiency.

RESPIRATORY TRACT INFECTION

Guinea pigs are susceptible to pneumonia and pleurisy. Visible symptoms include poor condition, coughing and rapid breathing. This occurs when the animal has been exposed to drafts and wet bedding and can result in death if not given attention. The best treatment is to clean the bedding, place a great deal of clean hay or cedar chips in the hospital cage and keep the animal out of all drafts, including those caused by air conditioning.

Pseudo Tuberculosis

Mothers may infect their young with the disease through nursing. The infection may prove acute and death will occur within days. If it is a chronic form the whole herd may be infected before you detect it. Visible symptoms include wasting, diarrhea, rapid breathing and coughing. The visible symptoms of this disease are very similar to diarrhea or to a common cold, so it is strongly recommended that you isolate the animal that is afflicted and take it to a veterinarian for correct diagnosis rather than risk guessing at the problem yourself.

Abscesses

These can be lanced by a veterinarian, drained and followed up with care and swabs of antiseptic.

Fighting

If the animals fight and wound each other with their kicking and nipping, the surrounding hair should be cut away and treated with antiseptic that has been diluted and applied to the *cuts and abrasions* as you would treat something on your own body. Watch to see that it does not start suppurating; it should not do this unless an infection has set in due to neglect.

Parasites

If you find that your pig has little white lice in its hair you can treat this with a mild flea powder marketed for kittens. You can either obtain such medication from your local animal hospital or from a pet shop. Dust the animal with the powder, taking care not to powder its eyes. Repeat this treatment once a week until you get rid of the lice.

Fleas and ticks have been carried in by you or a bigger animal and have then been transferred to the colony. This is your fault. Remove the fleas and ticks if you can or apply an aerocidal insecticide suitable for cats and cavies. Do not use the insecticides made for dogs as they can be too potent.

Most guinea pig health problems can be prevented by keeping the cavies in a warm, comfortable environment and giving them a proper diet. It is also important that they are each given enough territory (if kept in groups), so as to avoid any fighting. (1) A silver-gray agouti. (2) A tri-color agouti. (3) A black and white Abyssinian sow and her albino juvenile. (Right) A self-black and self-lilac peeking out of their transport box.

Scabies and other parasites besides lice and fleas can be dealt with in the same way as lice: use the mild powder Symptoms include scabby sores from these microscopic mites and constant scratching on the part of the pig (more than is usual).

Flies should be kept away from the breeding and housing area as they lay their eggs in the hair of the animal and when the maggots hatch, they dig themselves into the animal's skin. This is very bad especially for the young. Flies are much harder to eliminate than lice.

BREEDING PROBLEMS

Infertility can be caused by many factors including ill health, age, inbreeding that has been done excessively or a vitamin E deficiency (the so-called sex vitamin).

Premature births can result from the female or sow being bred too young, your manhandling of her, fighting, dirty surroundings, noise, a shock or any of the ailments mentioned above.

Stillbirths come from a prolonged and difficult labor.

Blindness is from excessive inbreeding as is *polydactylism* (a growth of an extra toe which is generally a recessive trait).

CONSTIPATION

The young may have a case of *constipation* which must not go unattended. This is caused by eating the food pellets without also drinking water. See that they have access to the sipper tube which may be out of their reach but which the adult can reach easily. Greens, an apple or lettuce can cure this as well as food that has been soaked in water.

HAIR PROBLEMS

If animals are bored or nervous they will chew their hair. This can be disastrous if it is a show animal and most particularly if it is one of the long-haired breeds like the

(1) It is often important to examine the teeth. Overgrown teeth are the result of not enough chewing matter for the guinea pig to gnaw. (2) A healthy litter will usually have 2 or 3 piglets.

Abyssinian, the Sheltie or the Peruvian. This may also be caused by a vitamin deficiency or a lack of fiber in the diet.

Half a teaspoon of cod liver oil or linseed oil will add a shine and luster to the animal's coat if the oil is spooned over the pellets.

If the hair of your animal seems to be shedding a great deal this is directly associated with an inadequate diet.

OTHER PROBLEMS

Overgrown teeth are the result of not enough chewing matter for the guinea pig to gnaw. Put cardboard tubes, a raw carrot or celery in the housing area or do not always soak the pellets. If the teeth grow too long the cavy will eventually not be able to close its mouth and chew at all. There is a good possibility that your cavy could starve to death if its teeth get too long.

If you drop your animal, watch to see if any *bones are broken.* The animal will either freeze and squeek, limp or appear uncoordinated. If it does, consult your veterinarian.

1

2

Health is especially important during your cavy's pregnancy and immediately after the piglets' birth. (1) This newborn piglet is less than 5 minutes old and is still wet. (2) Another newborn of the same litter, still wet, is already scratching and moving about the cage. (3) A sow with her week-old brood. Unlike many rodents, newborn guinea pigs can see and have hair. They are also less dependent on their mothers. (4) The same guinea pig from photo number 2, a tortoise-shell and white Abyssinian, 7 weeks later during its rapid growth period.

3

4

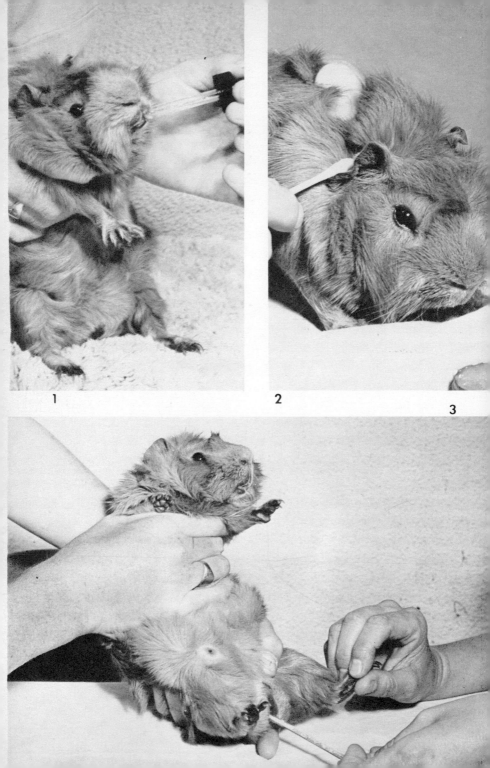

1

2

3

If you are in any doubt about what is wrong with your animal or you suspect something, isolate it from the rest of the colony or from its mate and keep it warm and its housing dry. Sweet smelling hay or mounds of cedar chips would be ideal. Then transport it to your veterinarian or local animal hospital for an accurate diagnosis and treatment. For less significant ailments, your local pet shop can give you advice.

DISPOSAL METHODS

The physical disposal method consists of breaking the animal's neck quickly and painlessly. The chemical disposal method consists of covering the bottom of a refuse bin with rags onto which you pour a few ounces of ether or chloroform. Over this you place some mesh to cover the rags and then you place the animals inside and keep the container airtight. The first method would apply to your pet and individual animals, while the second method would apply to many animals that had either a collective disease that would contaminate the rest of the colony or that you were using for experimentation in a school or college. These chemical substances are toxic for humans as well as these smaller mammals and great care must be exercised in using them.

Some aspects of guinea pig health care: (1) Feeding a cavy vitamins or medicine using an eyedropper. (2) Applying salve to cuts or bites on a cavy. (3) Taking a cavy's temperature. (4) Cavies may sometimes need shots. These should be administered by a veterinarian.

4

(1) Guinea pigs can be very affectionate and it is easy to become emotionally attached to them. (2) The author's albino Abyssinian would squeak if separated from her mate and not given any attention. (Right) Guinea pigs will eat almost any vegetable matter, including daisies.

1

2

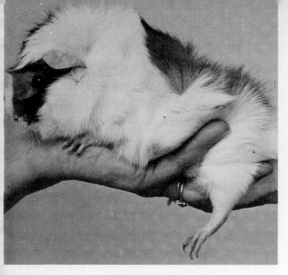

(Left) Healthy guinea pigs are a must for successful matings that will yield a good stock. (Below) A cavy show judge carefully examines a competing animal in order to assess the quality of its color, pattern and body shape, along with the overall health of the animal. Successful breeding that will yield champion stock requires a basic knowledge of genetics.

Genetics

Any serious breeder or hobbyist must deal with and fully understand the processes by which their guinea pigs acquire inherited physical traits. In other words, they should know the basic fundamentals of genetics. Genetics is a branch of biology that deals with the heredity and variation of organisms, and with the mechanisms by which these are effected. Its understanding will help you comprehend why there is such a variety of guinea pig colors and coat types and why the offspring of your animals may have different colors and coat types from those of their parents. These traits and many others are inherited factors.

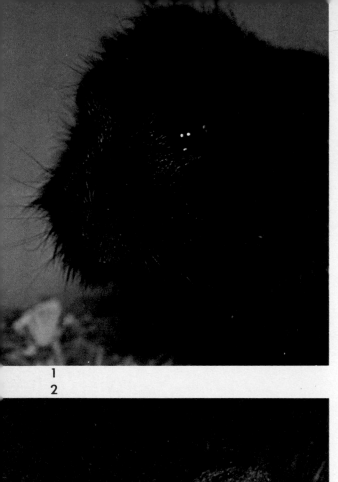

1

(1) A black Abyssinian boar. (2) The black boar's genital opening which houses his penis. (3) The testes are the paired round glands surrounded by the scrotum behind the penis. (4) The sow eats the afterbirth immediately. (5) These two newborn guinea pigs are less than 5 minutes old.

2

3

4

5

THE BASIC UNDERSTANDING

The term genetics comes from the word "gene." A gene is a complex protein molecule that transmits hereditary characters. In effect it is a blueprint for the entire organism. Genes are found in all animal cells. They are attached to long organic chemical strands called chromosomes. The chromosomes are passed from generation to generation during reproduction. Sexually reproducing animals have a diploid chromosome arrangement in their cells, diploid meaning that the chromosomes are paired. The sex cells of these animals, however, have a haploid chromosome arrangement, haploid meaning that the chromosomes are unpaired or single. Each parent of the sexually reproducing animal contributes a gamete, or sex cell, during the reproductive process. These two gametes unite to form a single unit which has a diploid number of chromosomes. In this way one of each pair of chromosomes is passed from parent to offspring, and these chromosomes carry the inherited factors on their genes. Thus these chromosomes with the genes attached carry the code of life which is passed from parent to offspring. This code exerts control over most of an organism's (in this case guinea pig) characteristics, including sex, color, size and general appearance. In most cases (except linkage which is discussed later), the parental chromosome passed to the offspring can be either of the two available (there is diploid number, remember?) and which of these two that is used is a matter of chance.

Most characters have several different forms. For example, your guinea pig may have brown, black or red eyes; it may have agouti, brown, red or some other colored hairs. Thus, the gene for, say, skin color can have several forms each of which exhibits a different color. When a particular gene has more than one form, the different forms are called alleles.

As stated earlier the genes are attached to chromosomes and these chromosomes are paired. A set of two genes will govern all or part of a trait. Often a trait will have several forms. The forms exhibited by the animal will depend upon the types of alleles that it has. Certain genes exert a controlling influence over others and are termed dominant while the latent genes are termed recessive. In the guinea pig, for example, the agouti color pattern is dominant over the other hair colors. Genes are given letters as names so that they can easily be referred to. Capital letters represent dominant alleles (gene form) and lower case letters represent intermediate or recessive alleles. The agouti color pattern's allele is represented by the letter "A". A capital letter is used for the allele (gene form) which carries the dominant agouti color pattern and a lower case "a" is used for the recessive allele which carries any other color pattern. Hence, every guinea pig must carry either no A allele, one or two, which would be represented respectively by aa, Aa, or AA. Because the agouti coloration allele A is dominant, both Aa and AA guinea pigs will exhibit the agouti coloration while aa guinea pigs will exhibit some other color pattern. In this case the recessive color pattern will be determined by a second set of genes which will "be free" to show themselves off by virtue of the fact that a dominant A allele is absent from the agouti determining genes. It should be noted that when there are two doses of the same allele (either AA or aa for example) the condition is termed homozygous; and when there is one each of two different alleles (Aa), the condition is termed heterozygous.

THE AGOUTI COLOR PATTERN

It is believed that the original wild guinea pig had an agouti color pattern. Today, however, we see guinea pigs in a vast variety of colors. These colors are thought to be one of the first mutations to have occurred in the domesticated guinea pig. A mutation is a significant and basic alteration

1

2

(1) An albino Abyssinian female with her newborn young. (2) The female gave birth to three young, which is usual for cavies. (3) One of the piglets nudging its mother for milk soon after birth. (4) The piglets stay close together for several hours following their birth.

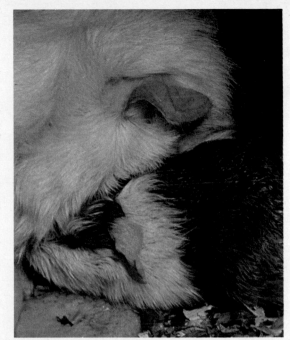

3

4

in the gene structure. It is a relatively permanent change involving either a physical change in the chromosome relations or in the genes themselves. This change usually occurs in the germ cells or gametes involved in sexual reproduction. Usually the mutation creates a change in the animal that is detrimental or even fatal to animals in the mammal group. Furthermore, mutants, as the mutated individuals are called, are often sterile and cannot reproduce. The color pattern mutation for the guinea pigs would have a negative value for animals in the wild. Their original color pattern acted as a camouflage while most of the mutant colors helped to set them apart from their environment and therefore make them more susceptible to predators. Thus under natural circumstances (and the Law of Natural Selection), these newly colored animals would have most probably been eliminated from the entire guinea pig population. This, obviously, did not happen because man took the guinea pigs from their wild environment and raised them away from their natural predators.

The agouti color pattern, as mentioned earlier, is dominant over all other hair colors. One would tend to think then that it would be most frequently seen. This, however, is not the case. There have been so many other color strains of guinea pigs developed that they have simply overwhelmed the original and dominant agouti coloration by sheer numbers of animals.

Perhaps you would have been able to see an agouti colored guinea pig. Each individual hair on the animal is banded with two or more different colors. The silver agouti is white and black, the brown agouti is white and brown, the golden agouti is red and black, and the cinnamon agouti is brown and gold. This banded pattern even extends onto the belly fur of the guinea pigs.

The agouti colored guinea pig has two basic pigment groups: brown/black and red/yellow/gold/white. The first group, brown/black, is called the ground color and can be either of the two colors. When the ground color is brown, the skin color is light brown and the eyes are dark red. When the ground color is black, the skin color is black and so are the eyes. The banding of the hairs results from a process in which the pigment producing cells switch on and off. This switch on, switch off, switch on action serves to band the hairs and functions throughout the life of the guinea pig. The ground color is switched on first and this is followed by the secondary color which shows itself in the switch off cycle. Since the agouti coloration is dominant to all other colors, a genotype (type of gene structure) of either *AA* or *Aa* will result in a phenotype (physical structure or result of genotype) of an agouti pattern.

THE NON-AGOUTI COLOR PATTERN

As was previously mentioned, agouti coloration is thought to be the wild and original guinea pig color. All other colorations are considered to be early mutations which were sustained by inbreeding the mutants of domesticated stock. Non-agouti colors include self-black, self-brown (chocolate), self-tan, self-dutch, self-golden and many more. These colors and a series of many different patterns are due to the interaction of several different genes that become "free" to show themselves off when there is a homozygous *aa* condition for the agouti determining genes. Below is a breakdown of some of the many genes studied for the domestic guinea pig.

The secondary solid color *E* series.

Some guinea pigs have a mixture of agouti coloration and a secondary solid color such as tan, red or yellow. The secondary coloration is due to genetic interaction from a second set of genes called the *E* series. The *E* series involves a dominant *E* and two recessives, *e* and *e^p*. When the phenotype is agouti *(AA* or *aa)*, any genotype involving the dominant allele *E* (either *EE, Ee,* or *Ee^p*) will yield the nor-

Unlike many other rodents, guinea pigs are born with body hair and open eyes. As newborns, they are much less dependent upon their parents. (1) This 2-week-old hamster has his eyes closed and still cannot see. (2) Newborn hamsters lack body hair. (3) Zebra mice, like most mice, are born naked, blind and helpless. (4) Newborn house mice. (5) The same house mice still have their eyes closed and are still blind after two weeks.

1

2

3

4

5

mal agouti pattern. However, *AA* or *aa* X *e^Pe^P* will give a patchwork of yellow, red or tan and agouti. *AA, Aa* or *aa* and *ee* gives a solid red, tan or yellow color. Furthermore, the *ee* genes inhibit all black and brown pigment. Generally speaking, *EE* animals are non-red and *Ee* or *Ee^P* ones have little, if any, red which would be noticeable on the extremities. Both *e^Pe^P* and *ee^P* guinea pigs have a good deal of yellow or red coat color and a degree of color pattern variation.

The color intensity *C* series.

The *C* gene group affects the color intensity in the guinea pig. Dominant *C* does not interfere with the intensity of the pigmentation. Thus, *AA* or *Aa* + *EE* + *CC* or *Cc* will be a normal golden agouti. The *c^d* recessive allele reduces the color intensity of the black and brown and has an even more subduing affect on red. The *c^r* recessive inhibits all yellow and red pigment. Thus, the guinea pig with an *E* allele and a *c^rc^r* complement will develop brown or black. *ee* or *e^Pe^P* animals with *c^rc^r* complements, however, will have white fur throughout with black or dark-red eyes.

The Himalayan form of the recessive series, *c^a*, inhibits all yellow and red coloration. It also inhibits the intensity of black and brown and restricts these colors to the extremities. Brown Himalayans and black Himalayans have coloration on their nose, ears and feet. When the *c^a c^a* gene condition is combined with the black-brown inhibiting *ee*, the result is a pure white coat with pink eyes. This would be, in fact, a true albino condition but for the dark skin around the nostrils, and on the ears and foot pads. This condition is often referred to as albinism, especially because of the bright pink eyes, but it is in fact not a complete inhibition of coloration.

The black/brown *B* gene.

Another gene which helps control color is the *B*, where

the dominant condition yields black skin and eyes. The recessive allele *b* yields brown skin and eyes. c^rc^r or c^dc^d combined with dominant *B* dilutes the black and combined with *bb* yields pink skin and eyes.

The *P* series diluting factors.

The *P* series contains a diluting factor where the dominant *P* yields normal hair, eye and skin color. *pp*, however, induces a light-red eye instead of the normal dark condition. *pp* also yields a silver shade from otherwise black hair, but it has no noticeable affect on the Himalayan condition. *pp* reduces brown to beige but has no effect on red or yellow pigments.

The white markings of the *S* series.

The recessives of the *s* gene series produce white markings. *SS* occurs in self- or uniform-colored animals. As there is not a complete dominance of *S* over *s*, *Ss* individuals usually have small white markings on their extremities. *ss* guinea pigs have white patches on the face and body and usually have white feet.

The whiting and recently discovered mutant *Rs* gene.

This gene represents a good example of the effect known as intermediate dominance. *RsRs* guinea pigs have an overall white coloration. The *rs* allele induces a roan coloration. Roan is a mixture of white with hairs of other colors. *Rsrs* guinea pigs have their normal color pattern interlaced with white and roan patches. Sometimes the feet and face also have white markings. Dalmatians are animals with solid or roan spots on a white background, and heavily roaned animals are called Dapples. This interaction is further complicated by the presence of a silvering allele *si*. This allele has a recessive behavior which causes a more uniform roan lacking white markings.

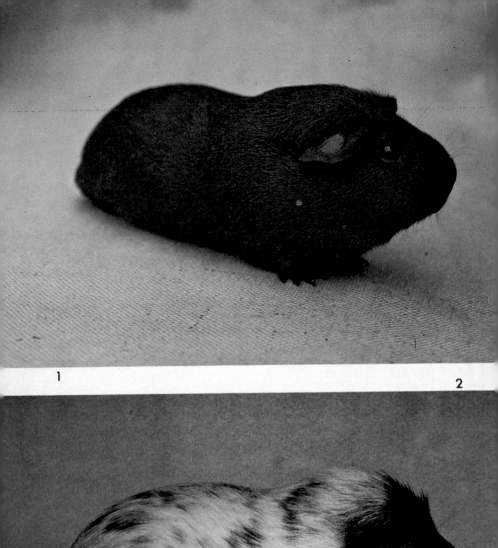

3   There are many different varieties of guinea pigs and this small book cannot possibly cover or picture all of them. The author has tried, however, to picture and discuss different varieties which are unusual. (1) The golden agouti, (2) the Dalmatian and (3) the American crested guinea pigs are not common in their pure form, but they are highly prized as attractive cavies.

HAIR TYPES: SHORT-HAIRED, PERUVIANS AND ABYSSINIANS

The three most common hair varieties in guinea pigs are the smooth short-hair, the Peruvian and the Abyssinian. The Peruvians are long-haired and the Abyssinians have medium length hair which is patterned with several rosettes on the animal's body. A fourth type of guinea pig coat called the smooth crested has a single rosette on the forehead and a smooth body coat. This variety is not as common as the other three. The forehead rosette is caused by a single dominant gene *(St)*. The combination of rosettes on the Abyssinians is caused by the interaction of two genes. One of these genes is dominant and called "rough," *R* and the other is recessive and called the "modifier," *m*. The expression of the two genes is dependent upon each other. For example, smooth short-haired guinea pigs may carry the *m* allele but lack *R*. Abyssinians with the most developed rosettes have the genotype *RRmm* or *Rrmm* and have well developed primary and secondary whorls on all parts of the body. Animals with only one recessive *m* allele have fewer and less developed rosettes. Often the animal just described will only have one rosette mid-dorsally with rough hair on other parts of the body. Lack of the recessive *m* allele yields an even less developed pattern. Peruvians also have a two gene interaction which expresses itself in a manner similar to that of the Abyssinian interaction.

It is possible to have an interaction where the guinea pig is the result of a mating between an Abyssinian and Peruvian, and the net result is an animal which will show the traits of both. One can easily see that the possible combinations of hair type and hair color alone can give rise to many complex patterns. Although this chapter has not covered all of the material available on guinea pig genetics, I have tried to touch on the most important aspects of the most commonly seen varieties of guinea pig. Below is a table with some of the most common types of guinea pig variations.

Phenotypes and Genotypes of Guinea Pig Fancy Varieties

Variety	Genotype
Abyssinian	$RRmm$
Albino	$c^a c^a ee$
Beige	$aabbpp$
Black	aa
Black-eyed white	$c^r c^r e$
Brindle	$aae^p e^p$
Chocolate	$aabb$
Cinnamon agouti	$bbc^r c^r$
Cream	$c^d c^d c^a c^a ee$
Dutch	$aass$
Golden agouti	AA
Himalayan	$aac^a c^a$
Lemon agouti	$c^d c^d$ or $bbc^d c^d$
Lilac	$aapp$
Orange agouti	bb
Peruvian	$llRRmm$
Red	ee
Roan	$sisi$ or $RsRs$
Salmon agouti	pp or $bbpp$
Self-golden	$eepp$
Sheltie	ll
Silver agouti	$c^r c^r$
Tortoise-shell	$aae^p e^p$
Tortoise-shell & white	$aae^p e^p ss$